ADVENTURES OF ALEXANDER SELKIRK

THE TRUE STORY OF
THE SURVIVAL OF THE
REAL ROBINSON CRUSOE

By

JOHN HOWELL

First pu

GW00685658

1

Read & Co.

Copyright © 2021 Read & Co. Travel

This edition is published by Read & Co. Travel,
an imprint of Read & Co.

British Library Cataloguing-in-Publication Data
A catalogue record for this book is available
from the British Library.

Read & Co. is part of Read Books Ltd.
For more information visit
www.readandcobooks.co.uk

CONTENTS

ALEXANDER SELKIRK

(1676–1721)

By George Atherton Aitken

Prototype of *Robinson Crusoe*, born in 1676, was the seventh son of John Selcraig, shoemaker, of Largo, Fifeshire, who had married Euphan Mackie in 1657. Encouraged by his mother, Selkirk—to use the form of name which he adopted—exhibited at an early age a strong wish to go to sea, but owing to his father's opposition he remained at home until 1695, when the parish records show that he was cited to appear before the session for indecent conduct in church. It was found, however, that he had gone to sea, and nothing more is known of him until 1701, when he was again at Largo, in trouble for quarrelling with his brothers, and was rebuked in the face of the congregation. Next year Selkirk sailed for England, and in May 1703 he joined Captain Dampier's privateering expedition to the South Seas. He must have had considerable previous experience, for he was appointed sailing-master on the Cinque Ports, of which Thomas Stradling became captain after the death of Charles Pickering. Various prizes were taken, and Stradling and Dampier parted. In September 1704 the Cinque Ports put into Juan Fernandez, and recovered two men who had accidentally been left on the island some months before. A quarrel with Stradling led Selkirk to resolve to leave the ship, and he was landed, with all his effects, on this uninhabited island. He at once saw the rashness of his conduct, but Stradling refused to take him on board again.

For many days Selkirk was in great distress; but as winter approached he set about building two huts, and in a few months he was reconciled to his lot. The island abounded in goats, and hunting became his chief amusement. After his powder was exhausted, he attained to great skill in running and climbing in pursuit of goats. He made clothes of goat-skins, and tamed cats and goats to be his companions. Knives were formed out of some old iron hoops. Twice ships came in sight, and Selkirk was perceived by one of them; but as this was a Spanish ship Selkirk hid himself, and the ship went on after firing some shots. At length the ships belonging to a new enterprise of Dampier touched at Juan Fernandez (31 Jan. 1709), and, Selkirk having drawn their attention by a fire, a boat was sent on shore and he was taken on board the Duke, commanded by Captain Woodes Rogers, who had Dampier as pilot. The character given Selkirk by Dampier caused him to be at once appointed mate. The ships set sail on 12 Feb. Several prizes were taken, and Selkirk was given the command of the Increase (29 March). In January 1710 he was made sailing-master of a new prize, under Captain Dover, and on 14 Oct. 1711, after a long delay at the Cape, they reached the Thames. Selkirk's booty was 800*l.*

Selkirk had been absent from England for over eight years, more than half of which he had spent on Juan Fernandez, and his adventures excited much interest when described in Captain Woodes

Rogers's *A Cruising Voyage round the World*, and Captain Edward Cooke's *A Voyage to the South Sea and round the World* (vol. ii. introduction), both published in 1712. There was also a catchpenny pamphlet, *Providence Displayed, or a Surprising Account of one Alexander Selkirk … written by his own hand* (reprinted in *Harl. Misc.*, 1810, v. 429). Selkirk was introduced to Steele, who knew Woodes Rogers (Aitken, *Life of Steele*, ii. 195–6), and his story was made the subject of a graphic paper (No. 26) in the *Englishman* (3 Dec. 1713). Steele describes him as a man of good sense, with a strong and serious but cheerful expression.

In 1719 Defoe published *Robinson Crusoe*. Perhaps Defoe's attention was recalled to Selkirk's story by the appearance of a second edition of Rogers's *Voyage* in 1718. Despite some apocryphal stories, there is nothing to show that Defoe knew anything of Selkirk beyond what had been published by Rogers, Cooke, and Steele. Defoe owed little of his detail to this 'downright sailor,' as Cooke put it, 'whose only study was to support himself during his confinement' (Wright, *Life of Defoe*, 1894, pp. 171–2, 402; Defoe's *Romances and Narratives*, ed. Aitken, 1895, vol. i. p. lii).

Selkirk returned to Largo early in the spring of 1712, and there lived the life of a recluse, making for the purposes of meditation a sort of cave in his father's garden. After a short time, however, he met a girl named Sophia Bruce, and persuaded her to elope with him, apparently to Bristol, and thence to London. The records of the court of queen's bench contain a process against 'Alexander Selkirke,' of the parish of St. Stephen, Bristol, for an assault on Richard Nettle, shipwright, on 23 Sept. 1713 (*Notes and Queries*, 2nd ser. xi. 246). In a will of January 1717–18 Selkirk called Sophia his 'loving friend, Sophia Bruce, of the Pall Mall, London, spinster,' and made her his executrix and heiress, leaving her, with remainder to his nephew Alexander, son of David Selkirk, a tanner of Largo, a house at Craigie Well, which his father had bequeathed to him (cf. *Scots Mag.* 1805, pt. ii. pp. 670–4). Selkirk apparently deserted Sophia afterwards. After his death, a Sophia Selcraig, who claimed without legal justification to be his widow (no date is given), applied for charity to the Rev. Samuel Say, a dissenting minister in Westminster (*Say Papers*, in the *Monthly Repository*, 1810, v. 531).

Meanwhile Selkirk had resumed his life as a sailor, and before 1720 seems to have married a widow named Frances Candis. On 12 Dec. 1720 he made a new will, describing himself as 'of Oarston [Plymstock, Devon], mate of his majesty's ship Weymouth.' He left everything he had to his wife Frances, whom he made his sole executrix. He entered the Weymouth as master's mate on 20 Oct. 1720, and apparently died on board next year. In the ship's pay-book he is entered as 'dead 12 Dec. 1721.' The will of 1720 was propounded for probate on 28 July 1722, and was proved by the widow on 5 Dec. 1723, when both her marriage to Selkirk and his death were admitted. She claimed the house at Craigie Well, and apparently obtained possession of it. Before December 1723, when she proved the will, she had married a third time, being then the 'wife of Francis Hall' (*Will of Alexander Selkirk,* 1720, in *New England Hist. and Gen. Reg.* October 1896, and with facsimile, *ib.* April 1897). Selkirk seems to have had no children.

Various relics were preserved by Selkirk's friends, and a bronze statue has been erected at Largo. A tablet in his memory was also placed, in 1868, near his look-out at Juan Fernandez, by Commodore Powell and the officers of H.M.S. Topaz, for which they were thanked by Thomas Selcraig, Selkirk's only collateral descendant, then living in Edinburgh (*Notes and Queries*, 4th ser. ii. 503, iii. 69). But the best memorials are *Robinson Crusoe* and Cowper's *Lines on Solitude*, beginning 'I am monarch of all I survey.'

A BIOGRAPHY FROM
Dictionary of National Biography,
1885-1900, Volume 51

" He never heard a sound more dismal than their parting oars."—p. 8.

ADVENTURES

OF

ALEXANDER SELKIRK.

———

ALEXANDER SELKIRK was born in the year 1676, and was the seventh son of John Selkirk, shoemaker and tanner, in Largo, Scotland. His mother looked upon him as one that would pass through some great events, and she resolved to have him push his fortune at sea, where he went in his nineteenth year, to escape the rebuke of his unruly conduct. He was from home six years; and again being guilty of very bad behavior, and having beaten a young infirm brother, and raised a riot in his father's house, he was publicly reprimanded: upon this, he left home, and being a skilful seaman, was appointed

Sailing Master, in a vessel called the Cinque Ports—a small sailor which went in company with captain Dampier to the South Sea.

Having quarrelled with his captain, and having had a dream that his ship would be wrecked, he resolved to quit it, and was set on shore at the uninhabited island of *Juan Fernandez.* He had scarcely left the boat, when he sorely repented, and he " never heard a sound more dismal than their parting oars."

From the beginning to the end of September, the vessel remained undergoing repairs. The disagreement, instead of being made up, became greater every day, and strengthened the resolution which Selkirk had made to leave the vessel. This was accordingly concluded on, and just before getting under way, he was landed with all his effects; and he leaped on shore with a faint sensation of freedom and joy. He shook hands with his comrades, and bade them adieu in a hearty manner, while the officer sat in the boat urging their return to the ship, which order they instantly obeyed; but no sooner did the sound of their oars, as they left the beach, fall on his ears, than the horrors of being left alone, cut off from all human society, perhaps forever, rushed

Selkirk catching Seals.

upon his mind. His heart sunk within him, and all his resolution failed. He rushed into the water, and implored them to return and take him on board with them. To all his entreaties his comrades turned a deaf ear, and even mocked his despair; denouncing the choice he had made of remaining upon the island, as rank mutiny, and describing his present situation as the most proper state for such a fellow, where his example would not affect others.

For many days after being left alone, Selkirk was under such great dejection of mind, that he never tasted food until urged by extreme hunger; nor did he go to sleep until he could watch no longer; but sat with his eyes fixed in the direction where he had seen his shipmates depart, fondly hoping that they would return and free him from his misery. Thus he remained seated upon his chest, until darkness shut out every object from his sight. Then did he close his weary eyes, but not in sleep; for morning found him still anxiously hoping the return of the vessel.

When urged by hunger, he fed upon seals and such shell-fish as he could pick up along the shore. The reason of this was the aversion he felt to leave the beach, and the care he took to save his powder. Though seals, and shell-fish were but sorry fare, his greatest cross was the want of salt and bread, which made him loathe his food until he got used to it.

It was in the beginning of October (1704,) which in those southern latitudes is the middle of spring, when nature appears in a thousand varieties of form and fragrance, quite unknown in northern climates; but the agitation of his mind, and the forlorn situation in which he was now placed, caused all its charms to be unregarded.

It was in this trying situation, when his mind, deprived of all outward occupation, was turned back upon itself, that the whole advantages of that great blessing, a religious education in his youth, was felt in its consoling influences, when every other hope and comfort had fled.

This circumstance ought to lead young people to prize their social and religious privileges, as they know not but that some day, like Selkirk, their lot may be cast far from home, and from pious family opportunities, the absence of which were then so much regretted by this lonely man.

By slow degrees he became easy to his fate; and as winter approached, he saw the necessity of procuring some kind of shelter from the weather; for even in that temperate climate, frost is common during the night, and snow is sometimes found upon the ground in the morning.

The building of a hut was the first thing that roused him to exertion; and his necessary absence from the shore gradually weaned his heart from that aim which had alone filled all his thoughts and proved a help of his obtaining that peace of mind he afterwards enjoyed; but it was eighteen months before he became fully composed, or could be one whole day absent from the beach, and from his usual hopeless watch for some vessel to relieve him from his melancholy situation.

During his stay, he built himself two huts with the wood of the pimento tree, and thatched them with a species of grass, that grows to the height of seven or eight feet upon the plains and smaller hills, and produces straw resembling that of oats. The one was much larger than the other, and situated near a spacious wood.

This he made his sleeping room, spreading the bed clothes he had brought on shore with him upon a frame of his own construction; and as those wore out, or were used for other purposes, he supplied their places with goat skins. His pimento bed-room he used also as his chapel; for here he kept up that simple but beautiful form of family worship which he had been accustomed to in his father's house. To distinguish the Sabbath, he kept an exact account of the days of every week and month, during the time he remained upon the island.

The smaller hut, which Selkirk had erected at some distance from the other, was used by him as a kitchen in which he dressed his victuals. The furniture was very scanty; but consisted of every convenience his island could afford. His most valuable article was the pot or kettle he had brought from the ship, to boil his meat in; the spit was his own handiwork, made of such wood as grew upon the island; the rest was suitable to his rudely built house. Around his dwelling browsed a parcel of goats remarkably tame, which he had taken when young, and lamed, but so as not to injure their health, while he kept down their speed. These he kept as a store, in the event of a sickness or any accident befalling him, that might prevent him from catching others; his sole method of doing which, was running them down by

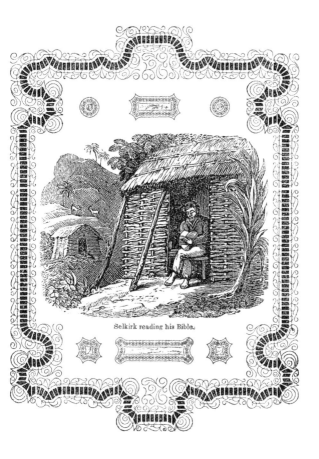

Selkirk reading his Bible.

speed of foot. The pimento wood, which burns very bright and clear served him both for fuel and candle. It gives out an agreeable perfume while burning.

He obtained fire after the Indian method, by rubbing two pieces of pimento wood together until they caught fire. This he did, as being ill able to spare any of his linen for tinder, time being of no value to him, and the labour rather an amusement. Having recovered his peace of mind, he began likewise to enjoy greater variety in his food, and was continually adding some new thing to his store. The craw-fish, many of which weighed eight or nine pounds, he broiled or boiled as his fancy led, seasoning it with pimento, (Jamaica pepper) and at length came to relish his food without salt.

As a substitute for bread, he used the cabbage-palm, which was plenty on the island; turnips, or their tops, and likewise a species of parsnip, of good taste and flavor. He had also Sicilian radishes and watercresses, which he found in the neighboring brooks, as well as many other vegetables found on the island, which he ate with his fish or goat's flesh.

Having food in abundance, and the climate being healthy and pleasant, in about eighteen months he be came easy in his situation. The time hung no longer heavy upon his hands. His devotions and frequent study of the Scriptures, soothed and elevated his mind: and this, coupled with the vigor of his health, and a constant serene sky, and temperate air, rendered his life one continual feast. His feelings were now as joyful as they had before been sorrowful. He took delight in every thing around him; fixed up the hut in which he lay, with fragrant branches, cut from a spacious wood, on the side of which it was situated, and thereby formed a pleasant bower, fanned with continual breezes, soft and balmy as poets describe, which made his repose, after the fatigues of the chase, very gratifying.

Yet happy and contented as he became, there were cares that broke in upon his pleasing thoughts, as it were to place his situation on a level with that of other human beings; for it is the lot of man to care while he dwells on earth. During the early part of his residence, he was much annoyed by multitudes of rats, which gnawed his feet and other parts of his body, as he slept during the night. To remedy this evil, he caught and tamed after much exertion and patient toil, some of the cats that ran wild on the island. These new friends

Selkirk amusing himself with his Cats.

soon put the rats to flight, and became themselves the companions of his leisure hours. He amused himself by teaching them to dance, and do a number of antic feats. They multiplied so fast too, under his fostering hand, that they lay upon his bed, and upon the floor in great numbers: and although freed from his former troublesome visitors, yet, so strangely are we formed, that when one care is removed, another takes its place.

These very protectors became a source of great uneasiness to him: for the idea haunted his mind, and made him at times melancholy, that, after his death there would be no one to bury his remains, or to supply the cats with food, his body must be devoured by the very animals which he at present nourished for his convenience.

The island abounds in goats, which he shot while his powder lasted, and afterwards caught by speed of foot. At first he could only overtake kids: but latterly, so much did his frugal life, joined to air and exercise, improve his strength and habits of body, that he could run down the strongest goat on the island in a few minutes, and tossing it over his shoulders, carry it with ease to his hut. All the by-ways and easy parts of the mountains became familiar to him. He could bound from crag to crag, and slip down the precipices with confidence.

With these helps, hunting soon became his chief amusement. It was his custom, after running down the animals, to slit their ears, and then allow them to escape. The young he carried to the green lawn beside his hut, and employed his leisure hours in taming them. They in time supplied him with milk, and even with amusement, as he taught them as well as the cats to dance; and he often afterwards declared, that he never danced with a lighter heart, or greater spirit, any where, to the best of music, than he did to the sound of his own voice, with his dumb companions.

As the northern part of the island where Alexander lived, is composed of high craggy precipices, many of which are almost too hilly to climb, though generally covered with wood, the soil is loose and shallow, so that on the hills the largest trees soon perish for want of nourishment, and are then very easily overturned. This was the cause of the death of a seaman belonging to the Dutchess, who being on the high ground in search of goats, caught hold of a tree to aid his ascent,

Selkirk catching a Goat.

when it gave way and he rolled down the hill. In his fall he grasped another of considerable bulk, which likewise failed him, and he was thrown amongst the rocks and dashed to pieces. Mr. Butt also met with an accident, merely by leaning his back to a tree nearly as thick as himself, which stood upon a slope, almost without any hold of the soil.

Our adventurer, himself nearly lost his life from a similar cause. When pursuing a goat, he made a snatch at it on the brink of a precipice, of which he was not aware, as some bushes concealed it from them; the animal suddenly stopped; upon which he stretched forward his hand to seize it, when the branches gave way, and they both fell from a great height. Selkirk was so stunned and bruised by the fall, that he lay deprived of sensation and almost of life. Upon his recovery, he found the goat lying dead beneath him. This happened about a mile from his hut. Scarcely was he able to crawl to it when restored to his senses; and dreadful were his sufferings during the first two or three of the ten days that he was confined by the injury. This was the only disagreeable accident that befel him during his long residence on the island.

W. Rogers says that Selkirk lay above the goat deprived of sensation, for 24 hours; Sir R. Steele mentions three days. Selkirk, computed the length of time by the moon's growth from the last observation which he had made on the evening before his fall.

He occasionally amused himself by cutting upon the trees his name, and the date when he was left on the island, and at times added to the first the period of his continuance; so averse is man to be utterly forgotten by his fellow-man. Perishable as the material was upon which he wrought, still the idea was pleasing to his lonely mind, that when he should have ended his lonely life, some future navigator would learn from these rude memorials, Alexander Selkirk had lived and died upon the island. He had no materials for writing wherewith to trace a more ample record. Upon Lord Anson's arrival, however at Juan Fernandez, in the year 1741, there was not, so far as he observed, one of these names or dates to be discovered upon any of the trees.

Abbe Raynal is not correct, when he says that Selkirk lost his speech while upon the island. All that Cook asserts is, that, at his first coming on board, he spoke his words as it were by halves, from want of practice; while he states distinctly, that he carried on conversation from the first and that his hesitating manner gradually wore off.

As to his clothing it was very rude. Shoes he had none, as they were soon worn out. This gave him very little concern, and he never troubled himself in contriving any thing to supply their place. As his other clothes decayed, he dried the skins of the goats he had killed, to make into garments, sewing them with slender thongs of leather, which he cut for the purpose, and using a sharp nail for a needle. In this way he made for himself a cap, jacket, and short breeches. The hair being left upon the skin, gave him a very strange appearance; but in this dress he ran through the underwood, and received as little injury as the animal he pursued. Having linen cloth with him, he made it into shirts, sewing them by means of his nail, and the thread of his worsted stockings, which he untwisted for that purpose. Thus rudely equipped, he thought his wants sufficiently supplied, fashion having no longer any rule over him. His goats and cats being his sole companions, he was at least neighbor-like, and looked as wild as they; his beard was of great length, as it had been untouched since he left the ship. Still his mind was at ease, and he danced and sang amongst his dumb companions, for hours together; perhaps as happy a man, nay happier, than the gayest ball-room could have presented, in the most civilized country upon earth.

One day, in his ramble along the beach, he found a few iron hoops, which had been left by some vessel, as unworthy to be taken away. This was to him a discovery that imparted more joy than if he had found a treasure of gold or silver; for with them he made knives when his own was worn out, and bad as they were, they stood him in great stead. One of them, which he had used as a chopper, was about two feet in length, and was long kept as a curiosity, at the Golden Head Coffee-house, near Buckingham Gate, in England. It had been changed from its original simple form, having when last seen, a buck's horn handle with some verses upon it.

Alexander Selkirk, at different times during his stay, saw vessels pass the island; but only two ever came to an anchor. At these times he concealed himself; but,

Selkirk fired upon by the Spaniards.

being anxious on one occasion to learn whether the ship was French or Spanish, he approached too near, and was perceived. A pursuit immediately commenced, and several shots were fired in the direction in which he fled; but fortunately none of them took effect, and he got up into a tree unobserved. His pursuers stopped near it, and killed several of his goats, but the vessel soon left the island. Cook says, "The prize being so inconsiderable, it is likely they thought it not worth while to be at great trouble to find it." Had they been French, Alexander would have given himself up to them; but, being Spaniards, he chose rather to stay upon the island, and run the risk of dying alone, and even of being devoured by his own cats, than fall into their hands, as they would, as he supposed, either have murdered him in cold blood, or caused him to linger out a life of misery in the mines of Peru or Mexico, unless he chose to profess himself a Roman Catholic, and even then he would have been compelled to pass his weary days in one of their coasting vessels in the Pacific Ocean; for as we have already mentioned, it was one of their maxims never to allow an Englishman to return to Europe, who had gained any knowledge of the South Seas.

This adventure made him resolve to use more caution in future; never a day passed but he anxiously looked out for some sail over the vast expanse of ocean that lay before him; for, even in all his tranquillity and peace of mind, the wish to leave the island never entirely ceased to occupy his thoughts, and he would still have hailed the arrival of an English ship with rapture.

On the 31st of January, 1709, behold! two English ships *did* heave in sight of Alexander Selkirk's dominions who was as usual, anxiously watching the watery waste. Slowly the vessels rose into view, and he could scarcely believe the sight real; for often had he been deceived before. They gradually approached the island, and he at length ascertained them to be English. Great was the tumult of passion that rose in his mind; but the love of home overpowered them all. It was late in the afternoon when they first came in sight, and lest they should sail again without knowing that there was a person on the island, he prepared a quantity of wood to burn as soon as it was dark. He kept his eyes fixed upon them until night fall, and then kindled his fire, and kept it up till morning dawned. His hopes and fears having banished all desire for sleep, he employed

"Slowly the vessels rose into view."

Selkirk running to the boat.

himself in killing several goats, and in preparing an entertainment for his expected guests, knowing how acceptable it would be to them after their long run, with nothing but salt provision to live upon.

When the day at length opened, he still saw them, but at a distance from the shore. His fire had caused great wonder on board, for they knew the island to be uninhabited, and supposed the light to have proceeded from some French ships at anchor, with which nation, England was then at war. In this conclusion they prepared for action, as they must either fight or want water and other refreshments, and stood to their quarters all night ready to engage ; but, not perceiving any vessel, they next day, about noon, sent a boat on shore, with Capt. Dover, Mr. Fry, and six men, all armed, to ascertain the cause of the fire, and to see that all was safe.

Alexander saw the boat leave the Duke, and pull for the beach. He ran down joyfully to meet his countrymen, and to hear once more the human voice. He took in his hand a piece of linen tied upon a small pole as a flag, which he waved as they drew near, to attract their attention. At length he heard them call to him, inquiring for a good place to land, which he pointed out, and flying as swift as a deer towards it, arrived first, where he stood ready to receive them as they stepped on shore. He embraced them by turns; but his joy was too great for utterance, while their astonishment at his strange appearance, struck them dumb. He had at this time his last shirt upon his back : his feet and legs were bare, his thighs and body covered with the skins of wild animals. His beard, which had not been shaved for four years and four months, was of a great length, while a rough goat's-skin cap covered his head. He appeared to them as wild as the first owners of the skins which he wore. At length they began to converse, and he invited them to his hut : but its access was so very intricate, that only Captain Fry went with him over the rocks which led to it. When Alexander had entertained him in the best manner he could, they returned to the boat, our hero bearing a quantity of his roasted goat's-flesh, for the refreshment of the crew. During their repast, he gave them an account of his adventures and stay upon the island, at which they were much surprised. Captains Dover and Fry invited him to come on board ; but he declined their invitation, until they had satisfied him that Dampier had no com-

mand in this expedition; after which he gave a reluctant consent.

So great was his aversion to Dampier as a commander after the experience he had of him, that he would rather have remained upon his island, its lonely possessor, now that he was reconciled to his fate, than have endured the hardships and trials he had before experienced under that navigator. This feeling must have arisen, not from any quarrel or personal dislike to Dampier, but from a knowledge of his former misconduct in his adventures, arising from his want of constancy in carrying through any object which he professed to have in view.

When he came on board the Duke, Dampier gave him an excellent character, telling Captain Rogers that Selkirk had been the best man on board the Cinque Ports. Upon this recommendation, he was immediately engaged on board the Duke. In the afternoon, the ships were cleared, the sails bent and taken on shore to be mended, and to make tents for the sick men. Selkirk's strength and vigor were of great service to them. He caught two goats in the afternoon. They sent along with him their swiftest runners and a bull-dog; but these he soon left far behind, and tired out. He himself, to the astonishment of the whole crew, brought the two goats upon his back to the tents.

The two captains remained at the island until the 12th of the month, busy refitting their ships, and getting on board what stores they could obtain. During these ten days, Alexander was their huntsman, and procured them fresh meat. At length all being ready, they set sail, when a new series of difficulties of another kind, annoyed Selkirk, similar to those he had felt at his arrival upon the island. The salt food he could not relish for a long time, having so long discontinued the use of it; for which reason he lived upon biscuit and water. Spirits he did not like from the same cause; and besides he was afraid of falling into intemperance, for his religious impressions were as yet strong. From the confirmed habit of living alone, he kept very much to himself, and said little. This frame of mind, and a serious countenance, continued longer than could have been expected. Even for some time after his return to England, these qualities were remarkable, and drew the notice of those to whose company he was introduced. Shoes gave him great uneasiness when he first came on board. He had been so long without them, that they made his feet swell, and crippled his movements; but this wore off by degrees, and he became once more reconciled to their use. In other respects he gradually resumed his old habits as a seaman, but without the vices which sometimes attach to the profession. He rigidly abstained from profane oaths, and was much respected by both captains, as well on account of his singular adventure, as of his skill and good conduct; for, having had his books with him, he had improved himself much in navigation during his solitude.

The articles he took on shore from the Cinque Ports, were the following: His chest, containing his clothes and a quantity of linen, now all spent, his musket, which he brought home with him; a pound of powder, and balls in proportion; a hatchet and some tools; a knife; a pewter kettle; his flip-can which he conveyed to Scotland, (at present in the possession of John Selcraig, his great-grand-nephew;) a few pounds of tobacco; the Holy Bible; some devotional pieces, and one or two books on navigation, with his mathematical instruments.

In the capacity of mate, he cruised about for a time,

during which several prizes were taken, and on his return to London, after an absence of eight years, one month and three days, he found himself in possession of £800 sterling. As soon as this sum was realized, he set out for Largo, and arrived in the spring of 1712, at his native village.

It was in the forenoon of a Sabbath day, when all were at church, that he knocked at the door of his paternal dwelling, but found not those whom his heart yearned to see, and his soul longed to embrace. He set out for church, prompted by his piety and his love for his parents; for great was the change that had taken place in his feelings since he had last been within its walls. As soon as he entered and sat down, all eyes were upon him, for such a personage, perhaps, had seldom been seen within the church at Largo. He was elegantly dressed in gold laced clothes; besides, he was a stranger, which in a country church, is matter of attention to the hearers at all times. But his manner and appearance would have attracted the notice of more observing spectators.—After remaining some time engaged in devotion, his eyes were ever turning to where his parents and brothers sat, while theirs as often met his gaze; still they

did not know him. At length his mother, whose thoughts perhaps at this time wandered to her long lost son, knew him, and uttering a cry of joy, could contain herself no longer. Even in the Meeting House, she rushed to his arms, unconscious of the impropriety of her conduct, and the interruption of the service. Alexander and his friends immediately retired to his father's house, to give free scope to their joy and congratulations.

A few days passed away happily in the society of his parents and friends; but from long habits, he soon felt averse to mixing in society, and was happiest when alone. Returning, therefore, frequently to Keil's Den, a secluded and lonely valley in the neighborhood, he spent most of his time in solitary wandering and meditation; till a new object began to engross much of his attention. In his musing by the burnside, he often met a young girl, tending a single cow, the property of her parents.

Her lonely occupation and innocent looks, made a deep impression upon him. He watched her for hours unseen, as she amused herself with the wild flowers she gathered, or chaunted her rural lays. At each meeting the impression became stronger, and he felt more interested in this modest female. At length he addressed himself to her, and they joined in conversation ; he had no avertion to commune with her for hours together, and began to imagine that he could live and be happy with a companion such as she. His fishing expeditions were now neglected. Even his cave became not so sweet a retreat. His mind led him to Keil's Den, and the amiable Sophia. He never mentioned this adventure and attachment to his friends ; for he felt ashamed, after his discourses to them, and the profession he had made of dislike to human society, to acknowledge that he was upon the point of marrying, and thereby plunging into the midst of worldly cares. But he was determined to marry Sophia, though as firmly resolved not to remain at home to be the subject of their jest. This resolution being formed, he soon persuaded the object of his choice, to elope with him, and bid adieu to the romantic glen.

After this elopement, nothing was heard of him for some years. At length, however, a gay widow, of the name of Frances Candis, or Candia, came to Largo, to claim the property left to him by his father, and produced documents to prove her right, from which it appeared that Sophia Bruce lived but a **very few years** after her marriage. He himself, after attaining the rank of Lieutenant, died on board his Majesty's ship **Weymouth**, some time in the year 1723.

POSTSCRIPT.

The chest and cup which Selkirk had with him on the island, are in the possession of a family in Nether Largo, in Fifeshire, who reside in the house in which he was born. The former is in excellent preservation although at least 123 years old. It is made of cedar, strongly built, and very massy. The initials **A. S.** are rudely carved on the lid. The cup is the shell of some kind of nut which probably grew on the island. The late Mr. Constable, of Edinburgh, caused it to be much adorned and beautified, by giving it a new pendicle, and having its edge surmounted with silver.—*Imperial Magazine.*

Verses supposed to be written by Alexander Selkirk, during his solitary abode in the Island of Juan Fernandez.

I am monarch of all I survey,
    My right there is none to dispute:
From the centre all round to the sea,
    I am lord of the fowl and the brute.
Oh solitude! where are the charms,
    That sages have seen in thy face?
Better dwell in the midst of alarms,
    Than reign in this horrible place.

I am out of humanity's reach;
    I must finish my journey alone:
Never hear the sweet music of speech;
    I start at the sound of my own.
The beasts that roam over the plain,
    My form with indifference see;
They are so unacquainted with man,
    Their tameness is shocking to me.

Society, friendship, and love,
    Divinely bestowed upon man,
Oh, had I the wings of a dove,
    How soon would I taste you again!

My sorrows I then might assuage,
  In the ways of religion and truth ;
Might learn from the wisdom of age,
  And be cheer'd by the sallies of youth.

Religion ! what treasure untold
  Resides in that heavenly word !
More precious than silver or gold,
  Or all that this earth can afford.
But the sound of the church-going bell,
  These vallies and rocks never heard;
Ne'er sigh'd at the sound of a knell,
  Or smil'd when a sabbath appear'd.

Ye winds that have made me your sport,
  Convey to this desolate shore,
Some cordial endearing report
  Of a land I shall visit no more.
My friends, do they now and then send
  A wish or a thought after me ?
O tell me I yet have a friend,
  Though a friend I am never to see.

How fleet is a glance of the mind !
  Compar'd with the speed of its flight,
The tempest itself lags behind,
  And the swift-wing'd arrows of light.

When I think of my own native land,
  In a moment I seem to be there;
But alas! recollection at hand
  Soon hurries me back to despair.

But the sea-fowl has gone to her nest,
  The beast is laid down in his lair;
Even here is a season of rest,
  And I to my cabin repair.
There's mercy in every place;
  And mercy—encouraging thought!
Gives even affliction a grace,
  And reconciles man to his lot.

COWPER,

Printed in Great Britain
by Amazon